CW01574549

freshresource

introduction&instructions

Experiencing Life is a discussion tool for small groups. It is targeted towards those who have no church background or experience. It will work with youth in most small group settings within homes, schools, churches, missions, and camps. This booklet covers three main values that everyone encounters in life: loving, giving and serving. The hope is that when someone is faced with a choice in life, after going through this course, they will have a reference to Jesus' life and the wisdom he has to offer.

The booklet is divided into 12 main areas of discussion and broken into three sections. Each session will open up a new story in the Bible and draw out good discussion from the participants. You will find each discussion will work best when three to twelve people are involved with an obvious leader to facilitate. The layout is designed to draw out opinions, feelings and thought patterns in a way that people can learn from one another and about one another. When possible, provide a copy for every individual to own and bring home. It is good when someone can follow along as it prevents a lot of surprises. Most people like to know what is likely to come next so having their own copy will assist in making them feel more comfortable.

The person leading the group needs to view his or her self as a discussion facilitator and not as a salesperson or teacher. It is vital to allow people to wrestle with their own thoughts and with their own view of Jesus and the Bible. This is not a tool to be used to 'close the deal', but rather to show people that Jesus is an example worth following. Be patient and allow the Holy Spirit to do his work. Be there to listen and learn from each other. The truth stands for itself, it does not need someone to reinforce its viability.

An icebreaker game has been included for the first week so that people can laugh together and get used to chatting and disclosing themselves in a safe environment. Use this game every four weeks or so to break things up or use another icebreaker to bring the right atmosphere of sharing. It is my hope that this is a life-transforming experience for you and your friends that will allow healthy community to form and love to be shared.

If you would like more materials for small groups and other settings, visit our website: www.freshresource.com.

Have fun. (Mark Dowds)

tableofcontents

experiencing life : written and developed by mark dowds and jason boucher
design and photography by joshua dunford (www.burnkit.com)
edited by jordan bateman. additional photography by adam neilson

check our website, http://www.freshresource.com, for notes, information, and help

» experiencing life

{loving} sectionone

topicone {gravitational pull} _10

topictwo {momentary beauty} _14

topicthree {everlasting} _18

topicfour {love has perspective} _22

{giving} sectiontwo

topicone {sight for sore eyes} _28

topictwo {picnic party} _32

topicthree {excessive compulsive} _36

topicfour {the green mile} _40

{serving} sectionthree

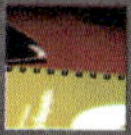
topicone {come on down} _46

topictwo {morpheus the man} _50

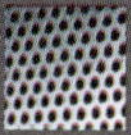
topicthree {shameless act} _54

topicfour {mr. nice guy} _58

ice {**breaker**}

This is a simple story-telling game to play with a small group of people. It revolves around using the statement 'I have never' and telling the truth. This is a game where you get to know one another in a bizarre sort of way.

How to play:
Everyone sits in a circle in the same room. Everyone but one person has a chair or pillow to sit on. The person without a seat stands in the middle and begins the game. The person standing shares a truth statement about himself or herself by saying, "I have never…" (e.g. "I have never been skydiving"). Everyone sitting then faces the truth. Anyone sitting that has done what the person standing has never done stands up and swaps places. When the place swapping is going on the person who was standing makes a break for an available place leaving someone else on the hot spot. The game continues by repeating this process.

An additional idea to make the game more interesting:
If only one person stands up they have to tell the story of when and where they did this unique act. Keep it brief so that the game doesn't drag on.

- There is no winner to the game - it is purely a fun experience and a good way to get to know the weird side of one another.
- The game works best with 10 - 15 people playing.

section one {loving}

"Jesus was God's exact replica."

–Phillip Yancey

topicone {gravitational pull}

Home is where the love is.

Icebreaker: If you were the lead singer in a famous pop group what would be your finale song and why?

The thought had been brewing inside for quite a while. His days were filled with dreaming and wondering of another life. Breaking free from it all, erasing the past, and venturing out on his own to make it without the help of anyone else, especially his dad. After all, if he just stayed were he was, life would still be the same in 10 years. Doing the same old thing, day in and day out. His brother would still bug him every moment of the day and he would be dependant on his dad until he died.

The stories of what it was like in the big city intrigued him. He was confident that he had what it took to make it out there. All he needed to do was go for it, take the risk, think about himself for once, and pursue his wildest dreams. He eventually made the choice; nothing was going to stand in his way. He went to his dad and asked if he could get his share of the inheritance early and, surprisingly enough, his dad went for it and divided up the farm appropriately. Shortly after this, he packed everything he owned, cashed in what he could, and made the move. He left nothing to come back to, as he was confident of his success in the city he was moving to. The new life turned out to be wild and dramatic, changing every moment. Every new day brought something different. There were no boundaries and no one to tell him what to do next. He was his own boss and did whatever he wanted, 24 hours a day. He had more money than he could ever have needed and money was everywhere in the city, there was no need for caution. Until one day when everything changed. The economy shifted and a famine hit the land. He lost everything he owned in what seemed to him like overnight.

He was forced to live in the dregs of society, feeding pigs in the hope that he could get some form of shelter and food. Nothing came his way, it only got worse. He was pushed to the end of himself, ripped of dreams and passion. All he was left with was the feeling of failure and hopelessness. One day, in the midst of despair, he came to his senses and realized if he just went home he could at least have a job, some food, and a place to sleep. He humbly got up and started to make his way home. His dad saw him coming in the distance and ran to meet him with tear-filled eyes. When they met, the son began to spill out his rehearsed speech of apology only to be silenced by his dad. His dad quickly got him a new wardrobe of clothes and pulled an extravagant party to celebrate his return.

Read more: Luke 15.11-32

- Have you ever screwed up like the guy in the story?
- How do you normally feel after really messing up?
- How do you normally recover after messing up?

One reason Jesus told this story was to give a glimpse into how God treats those who mess up. He makes the analogy of the dad being like God the Father.

- What would you have expected the dad to do in this story?
- What surprised you about how he treated his son when he came back?
- Why do you think that the Father accepted him back so easily?

God's love is full of grace. He understands immaturity and knows that there is no real life without him. He knows that if he is patient that people will eventually be faced with the fact that their big dreams are empty if they do not include him. He loves it when people come back to him even when they have messed up. He is where we find the love and acceptance we long for when we are at the other side of hopelessness.

- Is this glimpse into the nature of God different than you would have expected?
- Up until now, how have you viewed God?
- Have you considered that God may be very approachable and easy to talk to?

Jesus tells us in the Bible that everything he is and does is the same as God the Father. When you think of God, think of Jesus and how he treated people. He was friends with the people that most rejected. He loved those who had messed up lives and were far from being perfect. He came to help people who want to be helped and those that have significant issues in their lives. Jesus loves normal people. He does not assess our behavior before choosing to accept us. We can belong with Jesus just the way we are today.

List one characteristic you see in Jesus that you would like to have in your life:

- Is there something you have done that you are unsure Jesus would forgive?
- What do you think of the fact that Jesus loves you today?
- Is there an issue in your life that you struggle with that you would like Jesus to help you with?

(use this space to journal your thoughts)

Luke 15.11-32

topictwo {momentary beauty}

Love makes people feel special.

Icebreaker: What was one of the best days of your life?

Simon, a high profile religious leader in Capernaum, wanted a closer encounter with a controversial nomad named Jesus. He invited him over for dinner with a few other religious citizens but was careful enough not be seen as associated with him. He avoided the customary greeting and, in general, was quite rude to Jesus, who took it in his stride and reclined by the table laid out on the floor.

Dinner was underway and the nosey hosts were just getting a chance to ask their devious questions when a commotion erupted at the doorway. A known prostitute pushed her way into the room and made a beeline for Jesus. The other guests were shocked and disgusted. They pulled back from the table and squinted their judgmental faces as the reckless woman withdrew a bottle of perfume from her jacket. Before anyone could stop her, the woman started crying and soaked Jesus' feet with her tears. She poured the perfume she had previously used to attract other men to herself onto Jesus' feet. Without saying a word, she bent over and dried his feet with her unravelled hair. She continued to caress his feet with kisses, continuing her uncontrolled expression of emotion. Jesus didn't flinch. He took it all in, made her feel welcome, and gave her the uninterrupted moment she had always wanted. The moment that would make her feel special.

Read more: Luke 7.36-50

- How would you feel inside if you were in Jesus' shoes as the woman wept at your feet?
- How do you think you would react if one of the most rejected people in school started to talk with you when all the cool people were watching?

Jesus is often different than what we perceive him to be. Our perspective of Jesus is usually shaped by how religious people act. It is important to get to know him for yourself before making assumptions based on other people's actions and ideas.

- What do you think the other people in the room were thinking while watching this woman?
- What rumors do you think started to spread about Jesus?

If you have read other stories in the Bible, you will realize that this was not the first time Jesus had gained a bad reputation for himself. There were rumors going around that he was a greedy drunk and that he was not the sort of person respectable or religious people should be associated with. But Jesus seemed to care more about loving others than how anyone else viewed him.

- Have you ever had people spread rumors about you?
- How did it feel?

Rumors can significantly damage people. It is important to learn how to avoid spreading opinions and images of someone if it is not encouraging. Be careful not to presume that your opinion of someone is correct; instead think of ways to make him or her feel special.

- Why do you think Jesus was able to focus on the woman and ignore the others' judgment?
- Would you like to be able to act like Jesus did in this situation?

Jesus will not let anyone stop him from making someone feel loved and accepted. He gives people his undivided attention and is not distracted by trying to protect himself. He doesn't care what others call him as long as he has an opportunity to love the unloved. He knew the most important thing for this woman was for someone to recognize her heart and love her for who she was more than for what she had done. He understood her actions when she poured the perfume on his feet. She had found true love and was giving up on searching for anyone else's love. She did not need someone to tell her that what she had been doing was wrong; she just needed to see the genuine love that could bring her the fulfilment she really longed for.

List one characteristic you see in Jesus that you would like to have in your life:

- Is there someone who you are afraid to be seen with?
- Why do you not want to be seen with this person?
- What needs to take place for this to change?

(use this space to journal your thoughts)
Luke 7.36-50

topic**three** {**everlasting**}

Love never fails.

Icebreaker: If you only had one hour left to live, what would you buy with your last dollar?

A young leader ran up to Jesus and fell on his knees. He had desperation in his eyes while he blurted out the big question he needed an answer to: "What do I need to do to get eternal life?"

Jesus gave him an interesting response, probably the one he was expecting: "You know the commandments: 'do not murder, do not commit adultery, do not steal, do not lie, do not defraud, honor your father and mother'."

The young man knew there must be something more than this as he had kept these laws throughout his life and was still lacking something. He told Jesus that he lived this way since he was really young and looked at him for something more profound, something that had special relevance to him as an individual. Jesus looked at him and loved him. He saw the hunger for reality and the genuine desire to know the truth so Jesus cut to the chase and spoke directly into his life. Jesus saw that for this young man to be fulfilled there was something he had to let go of, something that was directing his life and stripping him of the life God had intended him to enjoy. Jesus said to him, "You're missing one piece. Go and sell everything you have and give it to the poor, and you will find the answer you are looking for." The young man's face fell. He knew he had heard the truth but it was too hard for him to act on. He had a lot of money and it seemed too scary to do what Jesus asked. He slowly got off his knees and walked away sad. Jesus stood and watched as the young man disappeared in the distance. He still loved him.

Read more: Mark 10.17-31

- Why do you think the young man came to consult Jesus in the first place?
- Do you think he was surprised by what Jesus told him?

Quite often we already know the right answers to our big questions and hope that someone gives us an easier way out when we ask them for advice. Big questions normally have simple answers that require an action from us that we struggle to act upon. Sometimes we need the time and space to evaluate what we want to do when we are faced with the truth about ourselves. Jesus understands this and is patient with us.

- What do you think it was about the young man that drew out Jesus' love for him?
- Do you think it was easy for Jesus to tell the young man what to do?

Jesus' approach is different than what we normally encounter with other people in life. He understands the importance of letting someone come to their own conclusions when faced with reality.

- Have you ever had a big question you needed answered about your life?
- Who did you go to?
- Were they able to be honest with you?
- What was your response?

It is important to gather a couple of wise people around you in life who can assist you to grow and help you to ask the big questions. Choose these people wisely and find out whom they consult when they want to make life-changing decisions.

- How do you think Jesus felt when the young man walked away?
- Have you ever had someone walk away from you?
- Were you able to continue to love and appreciate them?
- Why do you think it is important not to pressure people to make big choices?

Jesus values our choices and is patient with us, even when we choose to ignore good advice. His love for us is not conditional on us doing everything right and following his example in life. He knows that, over time, we will see that his advice and direction for us will make sense even if it means making the wrong decision sometimes. Trusting Jesus' direction grows through experience. The long-term results of following Jesus show that He always has our best interest in mind. Jesus offers a way that brings life but it often confronts the stubbornness of our present existence.

List one characteristic you see in Jesus that you would like to have in your life:

- Is there a big question that you know the right answer to but are struggling to act upon?
- Why is it still a struggle for you today?
- What would it take for you to make the right decision?

(use this space to journal your thoughts)

Mark 10.17-31

topicfour {love has perspective}

Love has perspective.

Icebreaker: Where would you go if someone gave you four weeks away and paid for it?

Life is not easy at the best of times. Jesus knew that only too well. He filled his days meeting people and helping them, healing people of their diseases, and setting people free from their addictions. When people heard he was in town, crowds gathered because there were so many in need of love and others who were looking for a fresh start in life.

Ten lepers came one day and Jesus healed them all, but only one came back to say thank you. That must have been difficult. People started to go with him everywhere he went, hoping to learn and understand more of the life he was teaching about. Not many gave him time to be alone, so he had to get up early or climb a mountain to get some peace and quiet. Jesus only did what was good but when you read the stories you realize that there were many people who seemed to hate him and would do things to make life difficult for him. On several occasions, they tried to harm him or kill him. People spread false rumors about him and told lies about things he said and did so that he would get in trouble with the authorities. Even his closest friends walked away from him, denied knowing him, and betrayed him. This is what he got for loving and helping people.

The highlight of this was when one of his closest friends set him up to be arrested for a small amount of money. The Roman soldiers took Jesus, stripped him, beat him, and put him on a crossed piece of wood, suspending him naked in front of everyone, until he died. Jesus' response to this in the midst of his excruciating pain was, "Father, forgive them, for they do not know what they are doing." Jesus had a long-term perspective. He knew why he was dying and the life that it would eventually bring. This perspective kept him loving in the face of rejection.

Read more: Luke 23.1-56

- Have you ever wondered why life is often tough?
- When life gets tough and messed up, who do you blame?

Sometimes people say things and do things unintentionally that hurt us. Sometimes people set out to harm us for no apparent reason. This part of life cannot be avoided. A lot of people try to find a life that has no pain or relational difficulty but no one ever really finds it. We need to learn how to face life rather than trying to avoid it.

- How do you handle the tough times in life?
- Who do you talk to?
- What do you do to avoid the pain?

It is not easy to continue to face life when it doesn't make sense. Jesus was able to continue to walk through his pain because he knew God had a plan for all people. He knew that most people acted out of misunderstanding and were trying to protect themselves. He was able to continue loving people even after they hurt him because he knew this was their only hope of having the life-change that they needed to become who they were designed to be.

- Have you ever been really hurt by someone else's actions?
- How did you respond to them?
- Did your response make things better?

Learning to turn the other cheek is not easy. It takes perspective and a genuine love to see others become better. We can never change someone else's behavior to what we think it should be. The best thing we can do is choose to love them and see the deeper beauty in their lives.

- Has anyone ever taken the time to point out the beauty in your life?
- How did it feel?
- Have you ever taken the time to notice the beauty in someone else's life?

Jesus loved people and always esteemed them by pointing out the beauty of their uniqueness. Jesus did not walk around the countryside, putting people down. He lifted them up and reminded them of the reason why God had created them. People who met Jesus dealt with the ugly side of life by learning to see the beautiful. This approach drew people to Jesus and he gave them the hope they longed for by taking their sin upon himself so that they could know the fullness of God's life.

List one characteristic you see in Jesus that you would like to have in your life:

- Take the time to think of someone you know needs to be encouraged and tell them about the beauty you see in them.
- Is there someone you need to forgive so that you can both move on to become the people you are designed to be?

(use this space to journal your thoughts)

Luke 23.1-56

section two {giving}

"It's not the mountain we conquer, but ourselves."

–Edmund Hillary
(the first person to climb Mount Everest)

topicone {sight for sore eyes}

Blind man.

Icebreaker: Imagine 20 years from now, you are surrounded by the most important people in your life. Who are they? And what are they doing?

One day, two blind men went out begging. Instead of going to their usual spot, they decided to make a trip to the big city, Jericho. This was no ordinary trip, nor would it bring about an ordinary outcome. Along their journey, they became quite tired and sat down by the side of the road. As they sat chatting, a noise in the distance began to distract them. Whatever it was, it was coming their way. As they wondered what was going on, they overheard some of the crowd, now gathering all around them, talking about this man "Jesus" and how he performed miracles and did so many amazing things.

These two men's hearts began to pump. Without seeing Jesus, they began to call out to him at the top of their lungs: "Jesus, have mercy on us," they shouted. The same crowd that had woken this dream within them were now telling them to be quiet. These two men ignored what the crowd was saying and kept shouting. Their persistence paid off, as Jesus stopped in front of them. He asked them an interesting question: "What do you want me to do for you?" They asked Jesus to heal them of their blindness. Jesus was moved with compassion, and he healed them that very moment. This was a road trip they would never forget.

Read more: Matthew 20:29-34

- How much attention do you place on the needs of others during a normal day in your life?

Sometimes we rely so heavily upon our strengths that we forget to look at life through our weaknesses. Using the above story, just think of how many people would have been in that crowd just "waiting" for Jesus to look at them, so they could get his attention. It is helpful to look at the world, yourself, or your friends sometimes through your weakness rather than your strength. In Sean Covey's book, *The 7 Habits of Highly Effective Teens*, he tells the story of Monica. "I used to live in California, where I had a lot of good friends. I didn't care about anybody new because I already had my friends and I thought that new people should deal with it in their own way. Then, when I moved, I was the new kid and wished that someone would care about me and make me part of their group of friends. I see things in a very different way now. I know what it feels like not to have any friends."

- What could be a strength in your life that you now consider a weakness?
- If you were to embrace that weakness, could you turn it into an opportunity for something amazing?

Persistence is another key that is illustrated in this story. These two guys persevered through all the negative vibes they were getting from those around them. It would have been so easy to cave in the face of peer pressure, but they chose to persevere.

- Name a time when you persevered in the face of peer pressure.
- Why did you persevere?
- Name a time when you buckled in the face of peer pressure.
- Why did you buckle?

I can remember sitting in class watching the unpopular kids get picked on by the popular ones. I can still feel how I felt during those awkward moments as someone's self esteem got driven into the ground. What do you do? Do you speak up and risk the crowd turning on you? Do you just ignore it? As in our story, sometimes we need to cry out when everyone else is telling us to be quiet.

- Have you ever stood up for someone?
- Have you ever remained silent when you should have spoken up?

List one characteristic you see in Jesus that you would like to have in your life:

There are four stages of personal development. 1) Being ignorant of any problems. 2) Knowing you have a problem, but not knowing what to do about it. 3) Knowing you have a problem and choosing to do something about it. 4) Mastering that specific problem.

- Have you identified any problems in your life as a result of this discussion?
- What is your plan to fix them?

(use this space to journal your thoughts)

Matthew 20.29-34

topictwo {picnic party}

God's Mathematics.

Icebreaker: If you found the courage to do one thing you have always been afraid of doing, what would you want it to be?

As each person passed by this young man's home, the excitement increased. He peeked his head out the front door and felt the electricity in the air. It was more intense than a group of 12-year-old girls awaiting an autograph from N*SYNC. As he reached down to get his shoes, and follow the crowd, he heard a familiar voice. It was his mom calling him to the kitchen. He explained everything he overheard the crowd saying and asked her for permission to go see this man "Jesus." His mom agreed and packed him a lunch of five loaves and two fish before sending him on his way.

When he arrived at the seashore venue, he pushed his way to the front of the crowd, only to overhear a conversation between Jesus and his close friends. They were talking about some sort of food shortage. This fine young lad, eager to help in any way he can, gave up his lunch knowing that it wasn't a lot but a start at least. No one could have ever predicted what happened next. Jesus took the loaves and fish, blessed them, broke them, and gave them to his disciples. They gave the food out to the crowd and, strangely enough, the food never ran out. After everyone had eaten, there were 12 baskets full of the leftover broken pieces.

Read more: Mark 6.33-44

- What part of this story stands out to you?
- What do you think was going through the minds of Jesus' friends?
- Why was Jesus even thinking about feeding these people?
- Do you think you would have given up your lunch without being asked?

Illustration: Give someone in the group a coin with the following instruction: This coin is yours on one condition, that you give it away in the next 30 seconds. Then inquire to the rest of the group who would like to get the coin. Once the original receiver gives away the coin to someone else in the group, have everyone sit down and go over the following questions:

- How much was "so and so" given?
- How much did they give away?

The answer seems obvious but the truth is they gave nothing. They simply transferred something that was given to them. True giving will cost you something. Jesus said, it is better to give than to receive.

- Why do you think giving is so difficult?
- Have you ever given something away that cost you something? How did it feel?
- Why do you think it is important for us to give things away?

When we see a need and give, God can use it more than we are aware. His mathematics are different than ours. He is able to make something that seems small to us be big for someone else. Most of us have a deep inner desire to give away something big. The reality of life is that if we wait dreaming of that day it will most likely never happen. Giving of what we have today is the most important thing. God multiplies everything we give to benefit other people.

List one characteristic you see in Jesus that you would like to have in your life:

- Can you identify someone who has a need that you could meet?
- Take the time to think of something that you could share this week to benefit a bunch of other people.

Ask God to make you more like Jesus and ask him to help you love those who are unloved.

(use this space to journal your thoughts)

Mark 6.33-44

topicthree {excessive compulsive}

Pour it out.

Icebreaker: If you could model in an advertising campaign which ad would you like to be in?

One day, as Jesus was passing through Bethany, he stopped to relax at a friend's house. All of a sudden, the door burst open and a woman came rushing into the room. The awkward silence of the moment was deafening. As the disciples, and the rest of the guests looked on in disgust, this woman pulled out a very extravagant gift. She was carrying a box of perfume, more expensive than one year's wages. This woman, oblivious to the mood surrounding her, took this box of perfume, opened it, and poured it out over Jesus' head. It was bad enough that she had burst into the house uninvited, but now she had gone too far by wasting this expensive perfume. After all, the perfume could have been sold to fund many other important ventures; feeding the poor, supporting the next trip, or research into the cause and cure of leprosy. Everyone began to criticize but Jesus accepted this moment and promised that it would never be forgotten.

Read more: Matthew 26.6-13

- Why do you think the woman's act was so offensive to those gathered in Simon's house that night?
- Why would this woman have done something like this?

Imagine it is your graduation year and you work your bottom off all year long. You get straight "A's" but instead of using those grades to get into the premier university of your choice, you choose to give it away. Now I know you can't give away grades, but you get the picture. You do not benefit for that year of hard work, but choose to pour it out on someone else. That is exactly what this woman did for Jesus. Extravagant giving is always memorable.

- Tell one story of how you felt when someone did something extravagant for you.
- What is more fun - giving or receiving a gift?
- How does it make you feel, on the inside, when you give?

Sometimes we think that we do not have much to give away. However, if the attitude of your heart is to be generous to others, you will be surprised at how many opportunities you will have to give someone a moment they will never forget.

- What do you think went through Jesus' mind while the perfume was being poured over his head?
- What do you think stopped Jesus from being critical and rational like the others in the room?

Giving someone a moment they will never forget does not always involve money. You can surprise people you know by washing their car, mowing their lawn, or scrubbing their windows. Sometimes it is even more fun to do it and not tell them. Years later, they will still wonder about who the random lawn cutter was.

List one characteristic you see in Jesus that you would like to have in your life:

- Think of someone you could surprise with a random act of generosity. Plan it out and give what you have to make it the most memorable.
- Have fun when thinking about being generous to others. Forget about the rational thoughts that flood through you mind. Laugh.

(use this space to journal your thoughts)

Matthew 26.6-13

topic**four** {**the green mile**}

Thank You For The Cross.

Icebreaker: If you could recover one toy or stuffed animal from your childhood, which one would you recover and why?

When you strip away all the religious garb and mystique surrounding the crucifixion of Jesus, all that is left is one man's quest to overcome evil with good. It seemed that the more junk that was poured out on Jesus, the more he shone. Put yourself in his shoes for a moment: you are falsely accused of a crime, the most trusted of your friends abandons you, and to top it all off, there is the intense physical, emotional, and mental pain of being tortured and executed.

Yet, through it all He was able to transcend these horrific events and deliver something inspiring. He is a man who never let the circumstances of life dictate his response. Instead, his response came out of his strong character. You see, for Jesus, giving was a way of life. As he hung on the cross, with all the circumstances swirling around him, he was able to look everyone in the eye and utter this powerful statement: "Father, forgive them, for they don't know what they are doing."

That is grace. His actions, coupled with that statement, embody the very spirit of giving.

Here is a thought for you. When is the last time you saw someone wearing a gold electric chair as a fashion statement around his or her neck? Or how about a set of syringes in respect for death by lethal injection? Well, from Britney Spears to Outkast, U2 to Marilyn Manson, the cross, another method of execution, has been adorned as a fashion statement. Think about it. One man, Jesus, was able to take something so grotesque and offensive and make it amazing. He was able to transcend all of the stereotypical responses, the disgust, and the memories of the cross and turn it into a symbol of hope and freedom. As Walter Wink says, "If Jesus had never lived, there is no imagination that could have ever invented him."

Read more: Matthew 27.1-66

- What does the word grace mean to you?
- Do you ever struggle to forgive people who hurt you?

It is so inspiring to read about what Jesus did on the cross, so much so that it puts our lives in perspective. Every one of us has gone through difficulties and trials. Yet, if we follow his example, those challenges in our lives can turn into opportunities. We just need to settle in our hearts to live lives that are full of giving, even when it hurts.

- Is there anyone you are not giving to because they did something to you?
- What do you think of when you see a cross?
- Why do you think it is such a powerful symbol?

The amazing gift of the cross is wrapped up in a single verse. This verse is touted on bumper stickers, held up at sporting events, and even adapted by the World Wrestling Federation.

- Read John 3.16

For God - the greatest lover,
So loved - the greatest degree,
The world - the greatest amount,
That he gave - the greatest act,
His only Son - the greatest gift,
That whoever - the greatest opportunity,
Believes - the greatest simplicity,
In him - the greatest person,
Shall not die - the greatest promise,
But - the greatest difference,
Have - the greatest certainty,
Never-ending life - the greatest possession.

- What do you think when you see this verse posted everywhere?
- Have you ever thought of what it really means?

The book of Proverbs, found in the Old Testament, says that there is no greater love than to lay your life down for your friend. This is exactly what Jesus did for us. He laid down his life, so that we can know what life really is. He gave so that we might receive.

- What do you think about what Jesus did for you?
- Do you ever wonder why He had to die?

List one characteristic you see in Jesus that you would like to have in your life:

(use this space to journal your thoughts)

Matthew 27.1-66

section**three** {**serving**}

“How come they don’t make perfume that smells like dough frying.”

–Homer Simpson

topicone {come on down}

Come on down.

Icebreaker: What was the first CD you ever bought and why?

He wasn't going to give up easy. One more go, he thought, as he scrambled to grab the lowest branch on the tree. Some days it had its advantages but today, being knee high to a grasshopper was not helping him much. He caught on, pulled himself up, and scrambled to a place in the tree where he could see above everyone else standing in the crowd. On a normal day, he tried to navigate through town without being noticed by anyone, as his job as a tax collector didn't earn him a lot of favor with most people.

Today was different, though. He wanted to be seen and he was determined that being vertically challenged wasn't going to stop him. The people were gathered to see Jesus. He was passing through the city and didn't appear to have plans to stop anywhere. There wasn't a lot of room to move in the claustrophobic, roaming crowd. It seemed like everyone wanted to spend time with Jesus and hear what he had to say. Jesus paused, and in what seemed like a random moment, looked up at the tree and said, "Zacchaeus, come on down because I have to stay at your house today." Zacchaeus sat like a stunned bird on its perch, wondering if he was dreaming. The smell of the sweaty crowd quickly reminded him that this was reality, so he gathered himself together and shimmied his way down to meet Jesus. His heart was pounding as they walked through the staring crowd. They arrived at Zacchaeus' house and he made Jesus feel at home. The crowd was left talking amongst themselves, forming judgments of whom Jesus had chosen to socialize with. But this was a strange experience for Zacchaeus as it was first time he had felt accepted by anyone in a long time. He had been dying to unload everything that was going on inside him, but no one gave him the permission to speak like Jesus did that day. It didn't take long before he spilled his guts about how he had fleeced people and been dishonest about the taxes he collected. He felt awful and was full of regret. Jesus just listened and before anything else could be said, Zacchaeus announced that he was making some changes. He wanted out of the hole he had dug for himself. He told Jesus that from that moment on, he was going to pay everyone back - four times the amount he had stolen - and he was going to give away half of what he owned to the poor.

Read more: Luke 19.1-10

•Have you ever fought your way through a crowd to see someone famous?
•What famous person would you like to be recognized by in a large crowd?

Being a tax collector was the bottom rung of the corporate ladder in Zacchaeus' society. It was the first step that a person could take on his way to becoming powerful and wealthy over a long period of time. It was a tough job and it almost necessitated ruthlessness and dishonesty to survive and be recognized. The tax collectors were not liked by anyone and were renowned for their dodgy schemes and harsh tactics that made life difficult for the poor.

- What career do you think you might like to pursue in your life?
- What does success look like to you?
- How will you determine your own success?

Zacchaeus had obviously begun to make it financially or he would not have made a big deal of giving away half of what he owned. It looked like living the life he had always dreamed of was not working out quite the way he had imagined.

- What mistakes do you think Zacchaeus made along the way?
- What realization do you think he was coming to prior to meeting Jesus?

When we live for money or our own dreams, we end up walking over people and using them inappropriately. This only ever leads to a lonely, unfulfilled life. What does it profit anybody if they get all the toys in the world but lose their identity and all their friends?

- What do you think Zacchaeus was longing for most in his life?
- Why do you think Jesus made the time for him?
- What made Zacchaeus take the step into dramatic life change?

Jesus knew the best way he could have served Zacchaeus was by simply taking the time to be his friend. By ignoring popular opinion and going to his home for dinner, Jesus was able to be an instrument of change by listening. Listening is a key part of serving and allows people to wrestle through their thoughts. Most people know what they want to change in their lives; they just need someone to stand beside them. Yet again, Jesus demonstrated that serving is more powerful than judging.

List one characteristic you see in Jesus that you would like to have in your life:

- Is there anyone you know who just needs someone who will take the time to listen?
- Is there someone you know who is rejected by everyone because of what they have done? How could you be of best help to that person?

(use this space to journal your thoughts)

Luke 19.1-10

topictwo {morpheus the man}

7 **Morpheus.**

Icebreaker: What was one of the strangest things about growing up in your neighborhood?

Jesus was out for a walk one day with his friends when it got pretty serious. Some days they wandered, played, and at the same time, helped many of those they met along the way. This day was a bit different. It was obvious that Jesus had something he wanted to say that he didn't want them to miss. It was as though he only had a short time left with one thing left to tell them. This moment intensified the words that came out of his mouth.

It all seemed a bit cryptic but they were getting the point. He started telling them of a day in the future when he would gather together everyone who ever lived. He would divide them into two groups, one on the left and one on the right. He would invite one of these groups to join him in a new kingdom that would be full of good things, sort of like a big happy place. As he told the story it sounded like these people would be surprised to be invited. It was as if they didn't understand why they would be so honored. Jesus responded to them by reminding them that when he was hungry, they fed him; and when he was thirsty, they brought him something to drink. When he was the stranger, they brought him into the group; when he needed clothes, they clothed him; when he was sick, they looked after him; and when he was in prison, they came to visit. These people were still perplexed and asked when they had done these things. Jesus's answer was simple but profound: "Whatever you did for the least of these people you did it for me."

7 Read more: Matthew 25.31-46

- How would you picture your happy place?
- What sort of Kingdom do you think Jesus was talking about?

Jesus sees everyone as family, united with a sense of togetherness rather than viewing humanity as a loose bunch of isolated people. If a child is hungry it is his child, it is him. If an old man is sick, it is his granddad, it is him. Jesus sees things a bit differently and knows that the problems of this world are our problems together. Time is not on a wall or a wristwatch to Jesus; it is just one great seamless season. One love, one mind, one heart and one soul. We are connected.

- How do you tend to treat those who are in need? Why?
- Do you ever feel drawn to stop the noise and just help someone?
- Tell a story of when you were moved to serve someone in need. How did it feel?

You don't have to go to the far side of the world to find people who are in need. In need of love, in need of support, in need of food, and in need of clothes. These people are found in camp, in school, in cities, and in your street.
Most disguise their need and don't make a fuss about it. It does not deny the fact that they need something or someone.

- Why do you think we find it so hard to respond to each other's needs?
- Why do we often ignore the pull to help people who are in need?
- What normally goes through your mind when you see a homeless person?

It takes someone to be secure in who they are to be identified with the weak and needy of society. Many people shy away in case someone identifies them with this needy person and thinks they are like them. Others are too busy driving after their own dreams or proudly presume that this person deserves to be where they are.

- Why do you think that this was one of the last teachings that Jesus ever gave?
- Do you ever wonder about how Jesus was able to serve so many people without seeming to own much?

Jesus was confident in who he was. He knew he was God and knew there was no higher ladder to climb. He had everything and was everything. Jesus knew that there was nothing greater than to become a servant when he came to earth because it is the best reflection of who God is. Jesus was unashamed to identify with any person in society. The labels others used didn't change who he was; neither did their rumors. He wanted everyone to see that life is found in serving others.

List one characteristic you see in Jesus that you would like to have in your life:

- Take some time to think about why you would be embarrassed to help certain people.
- Take time to reflect on your lifestyle and how much time you spend helping others.

(use this space to journal your thoughts)

Matthew 25.31-46

topicthree {shameless act}

Shameless.

Icebreaker: If you were to live somewhere else for three years where would it be?

It wasn't as if she liked the situation she found herself in. She just wanted some affection and thought she might find it with someone other than her husband. It wasn't a good situation at all, it was a big secret, and she didn't know how to stop the randomly planned meetings with this other man. Things had gone too far and it had all got way out of hand.

They met again and were right in the middle of their naked rendezvous when the door burst open. It was some of her lover's religious friends. They were angry and disgusted at what they saw. Before she knew it, she was dragged out of the building and escorted to the temple courts for her judgment. The religious leaders saw Jesus and thought it a prime opportunity to catch him off guard. They brought her over to where Jesus was sitting and made her stand in front of a group of people.

She was humiliated and felt the eyes of everyone cast shame on who she was. She was ashamed of herself and waited for the first stone to hit her (it was a common act to stone someone for breaking the law in those days). These leaders provoked Jesus to give his verdict. Jesus knew what they were trying to do. If he admitted she was guilty, the people would stone her to death. On the other hand, Jesus knew she was guilty so he could not deny the truth. They had set a trap for him.

Jesus paused and took his eyes off the woman to relieve some of the shame she felt. He stared at the ground and wrote in the sand with his finger. This agitated the accusers who started to put pressure on him. Jesus stood up and looked them in the eye, shifted the spotlight off the woman and said, "If any one of you is without sin, let him be the first to throw a stone at her." He bent down again and continued his scribbling on the ground. Initially there was an awkward silence, but then, one by one, these men lowered their heads and walked away. When Jesus finally looked up, there was no one left other than the woman. Jesus looked at her with grace and said, "Go now and leave your life of sin."

Read more: John 8.1-11

- What piece really stands out to you in this story?
- What do you think is really unfair about this story?
- What do you think you would have done if you were in Jesus' shoes?

Jesus was different from the other teachers. He did not come to judge and look down on people, he came to serve people and bring freedom from hopelessness. He wanted people to discover life. Jesus knew that judgment does not help anyone to change.

- Do you ever struggle with judging people?
- Have you ever been in a situation when everyone judged you for what you did wrong?
- How did it feel? Did it make you any better?

When we judge people, we can put labels on them that draw out their bad side. If we come to judge someone, all we will see is what we're looking for. We need to realize that we do not see everything and have a limited perception into every situation. We all have bias and lack the full truth in every situation.

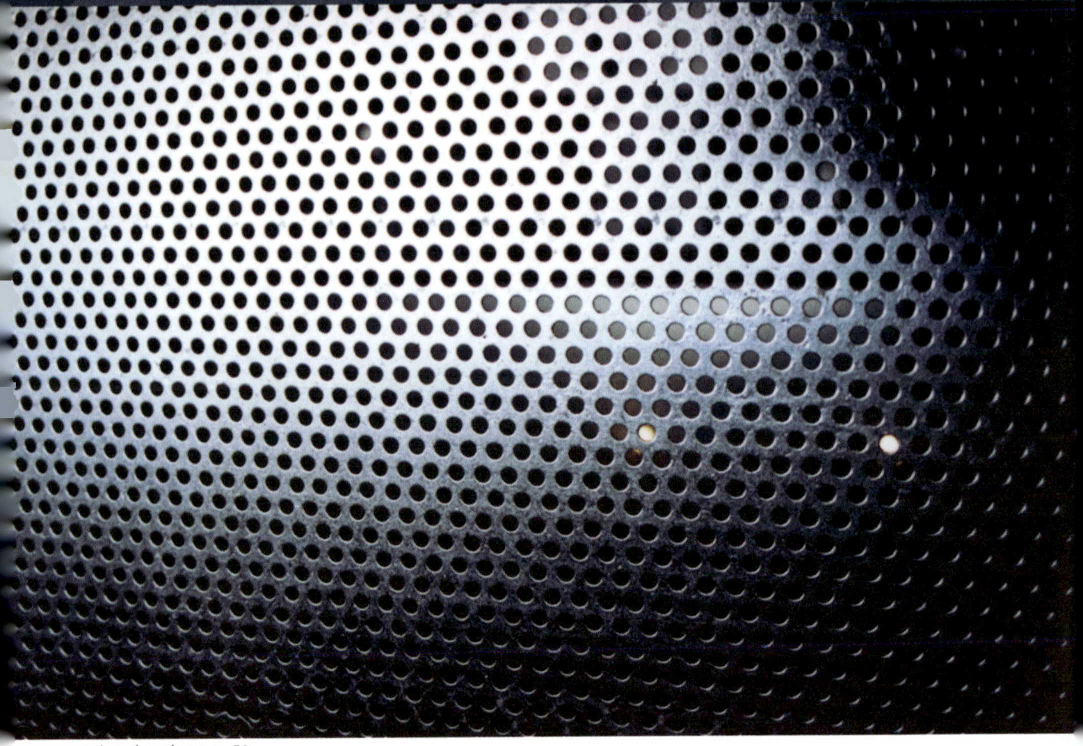

- Why do you think that the religious leaders did not bring the man she was with?
- What does this say about the people who brought the woman?

In every situation it is best to show love, grace, and a willingness to serve those who have gotten themselves into trouble. No one needs to hear that they are guilty, anyone who does wrong already knows. What they need is someone they can really trust to confide in, that can help them to make the right decisions to make the situation better. Love covers a multitude of sins.

- How do you think the outcome would have differed for this woman if Jesus had not shown grace and love?
- What perspective did Jesus bring to the situation with his few words?

None of us have lived anything close to a perfect life; we screw up all the time. Imagine if God was like Big Brother, watching our every move on a camera and chalking up our mistakes. Life would be mechanical and full of fear. We would never be good enough and would give up. Thankfully, God is not our Big Brother but our Big Daddy who knows who we are and loves us. Every action he makes is to encourage us to become who he made us to be and to draw us closer to him.

List one characteristic you see in Jesus that you would like to have in your life:

- Take time to think about why you really choose to judge people instead of serving them.
- Is there someone you need to go to say sorry to for making judgements on their lifestyle?

(use this space to journal your thoughts)

John 8.1-11

topicfour {mr. nice guy}

The Good Samaritan.

Icebreaker: If you were to act in a major movie, who would you choose as your supporting actor?

The road was just the same as any other day, but he had a strange feeling that someone was watching him. He knew the road and kept walking, ignoring his paranoid feelings.

The whack across the back of the head thundered his senses. Reality - and fists - struck him. He was getting mugged by a bunch of hoods. He was so stunned that the shock held him defenseless when they ripped off his clothes, stole everything he had, and beat him until he was almost dead. He lay there motionless, groaning, and unable to help himself. He could hear footsteps and saw the silhouette of a priest coming his way and a deep sense of hope entered his oozing bloodstream. Just when he thought he would feel the warm hand of help he got the cold shoulder of rejection when the priest ignored him and walked over to the other side of the road, leaving him helpless.

He felt this kick even deeper than the people who beat him to the state he lay in. Just when life seemed at its worst, another person came along. But he too crossed the road; walking the path the priest had previously blazed. The man resigned his mind to accept this lonely, undignified death. The noise of the road ebbed and flowed in his dulling mind. He was fading fast. The footsteps of a stranger approached but he accepted the inevitable, he was beyond hope.

He re-entered the conscious world while being bandaged and helped by a stranger. The man lifted him up to lie across his own donkey and took him to a safe place to recover. This busy businessman helped the man through recovery that evening at a local hotel and left an open tab for the man to get the best treatment necessary as he left the next day to continue his journey.

Read more: Luke 10.25-37

- Have you ever seen something horrific like this?
- How often do you think something like this happens in our society?

Jesus told this story in response to someone's question. Jesus had been teaching people to love their neighbor as themselves when an expert in the law confronted Jesus by asking, "And who is my neighbor?"

- Why do you think Jesus told him this story instead of giving him a straight answer?
- Why do think the man was asking this question?
- What conclusion do you think the man came to after hearing the story?

Jesus often told stories to show people how warped their thinking was. He needed to re-educate the way they viewed things. He knew this man was trying to work out whom he should serve and whom he should ignore. Jesus drew him to the reality that he was asking the wrong question. Jesus was showing him that it was more about him becoming a good neighbor rather than trying to work out who his neighbors were.

- Do you think this story is relevant to be told to people in today's culture?
- Do you think there are a lot of people asking the wrong questions today?

Almost everyone has a tendency to try and rationalize his or her behavior and to follow some sort of accepted standard. Jesus taught that life is not found in trying to follow a standard. He was more interested in bringing an internal change to people that would have an overflow into their normal lives. He wants to draw out the good stuff he has invested in us that brings real life and spontaneous acts of service.

- Is there anything about the story that surprises you?
- What do you think you would have done if you were walking along the road that day?
- What sort of things do you think would have been running though the priest's mind as he crossed to the other side of the road?

Quite often in life we ignore people who need help and presume someone else watching will help, or presume that there is someone more qualified than us that can help. When we see someone in trouble, our automatic response should be to pull over and meet the obvious need. We should presume that we are the only one who will help or we will rationalize reality away. The Bible teaches that we are the hands and feet of Jesus today. God is with those in trouble, waiting for a pair of hands to use. No business should become more important that helping someone in trouble.

List one characteristic you see in Jesus that you would like to have in your life:

- Take time to re-experience how you felt when someone helped when you were in trouble.

(use this space to journal your thoughts)

Luke 10.25-37

other **resources available**

Experiencing Life

Experiencing Life was developed as a discussion tool for small groups. It is targeted towards those who have no church background or experience. It will work with youth in most small group settings within homes, schools, churches, missions, and camps. This booklet covers three main values that everyone encounters in life: loving, giving, and serving. The hope is that when someone is faced with a choice in life, after going through this course, they will have a reference to Jesus' life and the wisdom he has to offer.

Exploring Christianity

Exploring Christianity is an eight-week course designed to assist young people who are leading their friends to God. It teaches some of the foundational truths of Christianity while removing common roadblocks along the way. This course introduces people to a small group discussion setting that in turn will lead to an easy transition into further community based discipleship.

Reaching Out

Reaching Out is a tool that has been specifically written to help young people understand the principles of peer-led small groups. It is an effective resource and reference for young people who are actively leading their friends through the process of discipleship. Reaching Out gives clear guidelines to follow that allows the leader to be effective and flexible while developing people in a small group environment.

Following Jesus

Following Jesus is a training booklet that leads young people through several stages of growth in discipleship. This resource helps to break down the strategy and mission of Christ into a concise process in which to follow. It details how Jesus ministered with people and emphasizes the calling of all believers to continue with the commission to multiply the life and mission of Jesus in society.

W2 : Live Worship

W2 is a live album that captures the experience of two Canadian bands that share one passion to worship God. It has a fresh and edgy feel to what is happening within the present evolution of worship among youth. The uniqueness of this album is expressed in the depth of lyrical poetry and creative use of popular instruments.

>> available at **www.freshresource.com**

freshresource